# MAÀ

**Truth, Justice, Order, Balance, Harmony, Reciprocity, and Love**

## POCKET EDITION

# Table of Contents

## INTRODUCTION

## MAÀT 42 PLUS GOD

**MAÀT is a rule of Law and Moral justice amongst the Ancient Khemet/Egyptians with the divine cosmological order within mythology, astronomy, and astrophysical studies. African metaphorical teachings about how human beings should live.**

**These injunctions of MAÀT were statements formed by Sages of the Ancient Kemetians and recorded on the Khemet temple walls and papyrus scrolls, which have survived to this day and time.**

**Negative Confessions, Concept, Principles of Truth, Justice, Order,**

Balance, Reciprocity, and Love are moral and ethical principles, which every Egyptian citizen was expected to follow throughout their daily lives. These principles are used for the sole purpose of cleansing personality deficits to promote true self-discovery throughout society.

MAÀT, known as "Prt m Hru" meant: The Utterance for Coming into the Light of the Highest.

These "Negative Confessions," Concepts or Principles were said to be 2000 years BEFORE the Biblical Ten Commandments.

If you study carefully, and WITHOUT criticism you will find similarities.

Biblical accounts refer to Moses as being an Egyptian who more likely than not, grew up worshipping Egyptian Gods and Goddesses. Moses to the Christians is Akhenaten to the Egyptians.

Maátian philosophy was the basis of the Ancient Kemetic Society and Government. It was considered the heart of Ancient Egyptian Myth and Spirituality.

The Goddess MAÀT was regarded as, a cosmic force and a living societal doctrine that promoted social harmony.

In India, the philosophy is Dharma, in Christianity, it was the Beatitudes, and the Ten Commandments in the Holy Bible.

For enlightenment, and not to offend anyone reading this book. The Bible is not a Holy Book. It is not divinely

inspired. It is a series of writings which are perverted fragments of ancient writings
from Kemet, and is less than 1,600 years old, while the writings of Kemet are over 20,000 years old.

The title Holy Bible is translated from Helios Byblos. The term Byblos is derived from the Papyrus which is derived from the papyrus plant used to make paper.

The term paper is derived from papyrus or pa-Pyrus[papers]. The term Helios is the Greek language perversion of the name of the God, Ra.

The Holy Bible or Helios Byblos or Helios Papyrus is a troglodyte perversion meaning, "The Papyrus of Helios or The Papers (book) of Ra."

**It is a series of plagiarisms, manipulations of a partial sacred text, and perversions describing the troglodyte's false worship of their fictional god.**

*"There are two roads traveled by humankind, those who seek to live Ma'at and those who seek to satisfy their animalistic passions."*

*- African Proverbs*

# The Negative Confessions:

- **I have not sinned.**

- **I have not committed robbery with violence.**

- **I have not stolen it.**

- **I have not slain men or women.**

- **I have not stolen food.**

- **I have not defrauded offerings.**

- **I have not stolen from God/Goddess.**

- **I have not told lies.**

- **I have not carried away food because no one is watching.**

- **I have not cursed.**

- I have not closed my ears to the truth.

- I have not committed adultery.

- I have not made anyone cry.

- I have not felt sorrow without reason.

- I have not assaulted anyone.

- I am not deceitful.

- I have not stolen anyone's land.

- I have not been an eavesdropper.

- I have not falsely accused anyone.

- I have not been angry without reason.

- I have not seduced anyone's wife.

- I have not polluted myself.

- I have not terrorized anyone.

- I have not disobeyed the Law.

- I have not been exclusively angry.

- I have not cursed a God/Goddess.

- I have not behaved with violence.

- I have not disrupted the peace.

- I have not acted hastily or without thought.

- I have not overstepped my boundaries of concern.

- I have not exaggerated my words when speaking.

- I have not worked evil.

- I have not used evil thoughts, words, or deeds.

- I have not polluted the water.

- I have not spoken angrily or arrogantly.

- I have not cursed anyone in thought, word, or deeds.

- I have not placed myself on a pedestal.

- I have not stolen what belongs to God/Goddess.

- I have not stolen from or disrespected the deceased.

- I have not taken food from a child.

- I have not acted with insolence.

- I have not destroyed property belonging to a God/Goddess

# MAÀT 42 PLUS GOD

*Human beings who deviate from MA`AT will likely meet with frustration, anxiety, pain, and sorrow.*

# THE PURPOSE OF LIVING THE WAY OF MAÀT

**The Purpose of these 42 Confessions, Laws, Principles, Admonitions to the Goddess MAÀT of Ancient Khemet of Justice and Truth, among the people of Lower and Upper Egypt was again to divert any chaos, Isfet, and perhaps promote social harmony and pave the way for Spiritual evolution in their society on many levels, even of today's society.**

**The Goddess MAÀT also personified as a goddess of the Stars, Seasons, and the Actions of Mortals and Deities, who brought order to**

the universe from the chaos of creation.

However, if these moral injections were memorized and never applied, never understood on a deeper Spiritual level, it was considered not being practiced correctly, or at all.

Maát's ideological partner was Isfet. Her duality, her opposite, the evil and troublesome one. When MAÀT wasn't practiced, there would be a decline in the Moral character of society.

When individuals would place more importance on worldly values, and not spiritual values of Life.

The oldest surviving record showing that Maát is the norm for nature and society, in this world and the next, is found in the pyramid text of Unas

(ca. 2375BCE and 2345BCE)

After her role in continuously preventing the universe from returning to chaos, her primary role in Egyptian mythology dealt with the weighing of souls (Weighing of the heart) that took place in the underworld, Duat.

The feather on her headdress was the measuring that decided whether the souls (considered to reside in the heart) of the departed would reach the paradise of the afterlife successfully.

Those with good and pure hearts were sent on to Aaru.

This book, " Maát 42 plus God" is NOT a history lesson, but rather to be perhaps viewed or considered a "Heart Lesson," to serve as a small guide to purifying one's heart and encouraging one to do further RESEARCH while living a life of integrity and good character.

African Spirituality DID NOT condemn others but, instead, it stressed keeping the PURITY OF YOUR OWN HEART.

Kill the enemy within, and the enemy without dies.

# MAÀT 42 PLUS GOD

*Human beings who deviate from MA`AT will likely meet with frustration, anxiety, pain, and sorrow.*

## ABOUT THE BOOK

This Pocket Edition of "MAÀT 42 Plus God," God meaning the totality of creation itself, gives ideas on how to incorporate the Laws of Maát principles in a more simplistic way for everyday living experience, in a reasonable approach fashioned for living a more prosperous life.

Fear not! MAÀT is not a Religion.

We must learn to manifest in a likeness and image of Truth, Justice, Order, Balance, Harmony, Peace, Reciprocity, and Love… and be undisturbed amid everyday chaos and confusion.

We must understand that it is in our best interest to always return to that truth, justice, order, balance, harmony, love, reciprocity, and peace daily as we go about the day. Learn to govern ourselves so we live together in a civilized social manner and build for tomorrow.

Ra Member, we are peaceful people by nature.

Our thoughts, feelings, and actions should line up with the attributes of and the reflection of the essence of God.

When your emotions have that response as of the energy powers of God, you will change all events in your life into positive experiences. You have the ability to create your day.

This book gives you a common-sense approach to everyday life experiences that will allow you to vibrate at a higher frequency above all negativity that one may experience throughout the day.

The Spirit of God flows through you to others.

Your emotions need to respond to Truth, Justice, Order, Balance, Harmony, Reciprocity, and Love to be Effective towards others.

You are a Divine Being.

MAÀT Ankhu MAÀT means MAÀT is the source of Life. Following these basic principles of Maát invites you to emulate the good, to have discipline in speech, hence prohibitions against quarreling.

Lying to and on others is a form of blasphemy. Listening emphatically to others with an excellent heart and doing what God loves is living "God-like." It is declaring innocents in both word and deed.

We are too, used as vessels for good, to be skillful and full of knowledge and free from negligence in distributing the knowledge. Practicing what we teach and fearful of being careless.

A Kind heart is your guide. Make sure your speech upholds God in you. Studying to show yourself approved being fearful of deficiency.

Do good business and never embezzle money. Let your conscience be your guide for your character alone will raise you above many.

Make your life purpose to live a life complete, whole and sound, and free from all that is hateful. Be a model for kindness because the favor of God lives within you and NEVER confuse the message with the "Messenger."

Remember, MA'AT is everywhere that you are.

One's heart is the seat of the God-consciousness and its sensitivity, presenting divine presence.

So, lead with the "God Consciousness" in your heart and be careful how you treat strangers, and be kind to everyone you meet. One must have a virtue of balance to ensure rational and emotional choices.

The heart plays a significant role in the Maatian moral and ethical discourse.

Ma'at is who you are.

Rise in the mornings with MA'AT and let every limb join with MA'AT allowing her to guide your actions throughout the day.

To express moral consciousness and understanding daily, one must develop ethical thought patterns which entail developing moral vocabulary and conceptualizing exhibiting virtues such as, sharp-mindedness, listening patiently, being hugely perceptive, and uprightness.

Living a life free from evil, in stressful situations always turning towards Ma'at, turning away from a liar, treating everyone with kindness, serving the needy, being a father to the fatherless, being a mother to the motherless, being a husband to the widow and refuge to the orphan, etc.

Adorations to goddess Ma'at, who is everywhere you are.

P.S. Before you criticize my efforts to spread enlightenment, first Innerstand why I am using the word "Eye" in the place of "I."

You will see the word "Eye" used in the place of "I," and the sole purpose is to help you to distance yourself from the Ego. The less

# Knowledge you have the greater your Ego will be.

# MAÀT 42 PLUS GOD

❖

# MAÀT 42 PLUS GOD

◈

## 42 PRINCIPLES OF MAÀT

### Eye Honor Virtue

**Honor: From Latin, "honos or honoris" means the evaluation of another.**

**Virtue: Behavior showing high moral standards**

**Living life in accord with reason and virtue is, living a life of purpose value, worth, respect, morality, integrity, dignity, decency, and nobility.**

**Virtue is an attempt to discover what perhaps is deemed as "good or moral character,"**

and to apply that moral character as the basis of one's choices to show good behavior.

(Examples of Virtue)

- Your moral barometer should tell you not to flirt or have intercourse with another man's wife or another woman's husband.

- Being Compassionate before Critical

- Your moral barometer should tell you not to sell drugs to underage people. Or sell drugs at all.

- Your moral barometer should tell you not to misuse or abuse another person spitefully.

- **Your moral barometer should tell you not to gossip about other people or spitefully divulge information that was entrusted to you.**

- **Your moral barometer should tell you not to steal that typing paper or miscellaneous items from your place of work, just because no one is watching.**

- **Your moral barometer should tell you not to blow your money on lottery tickets or at casinos when your children need food, clothing, and shelter.**

- **Your moral barometer should tell you not to have unprotected sex. Especially when you know you have multiple partners.**

- **Your moral barometer should tell you not to get that woman or man's phone number when you know that you are in a committed relationship.**

- **Your moral barometer should tell you to give your services or products away freely to those who are not able to pay IF, they are in a crisis and their finances are in a bind or reduce the price.**

   **(Barber, Hairstylist, Authors, etc.)**

**You must choose for your reasons, to listen to that moral barometer that is within everyone to use. Living by the principles of MAÀT will help train the ear to hear and the heart to listen to the essence of God within, the Universe, and the Ancestors.**

## Eye Benefit with Gratitude

**Gratitude: The quality of being thankful; readiness to show appreciation for the kindness, and to return the kindness shown.**

**Living life with a Cheerful outlook increases good emotional health. Giving thanks for all Life's blessings daily.**

**Practicing gratitude helps one's self-esteem as well. Appreciation is most beneficial when practiced. Perhaps, this can be life-altering by improving well-being by curbing depression and anxiety.**

**However, when suddenly life throws you a curve and people or things are abruptly taken away from you, can you still find gratitude in your heart?**

If you live a life where you are naturally appreciative of people, and all that you have then, life's little ups and downs won't have such a terrible and devastating effect on your emotions.

Because, you will know that with all that comes into your life, for a reason, lesson, or season… you are to be grateful for the embrace and the release. Ase'

You will cause yourself more pain resisting the enforced lifestyle change because, that gratefulness will turn into anger, self-pity, and eventually self-loathing.

There is joy everywhere you are but, pain and frustrations can quickly overshadow it if you allow it to.

## Eye Am Peaceful

**Peaceful: Free from disturbances.**

**Living a peaceful life requires Zen Habits.**

**Living a life of contentment and with ease, escapes the madness of it all.**

**"Whatever the task, do it slowly and with ease, in mindfulness, so as not to do any task to get them over quickly. Resolve to each task in a relaxed and stress-free way with all of your attention."**

**- Thich Nhat Hanh, Zen Master**

**Peace is not a day full of madness, where you are stressed out from the grind and the chaos of the business of the day.**

**It is not about the hustle and bustle but, rather enjoying each activity each day. Staying in the moment and being present and enthusiastic rather than rushing to finish things.**

## Eye Respect the Property of Others

**Understanding the importance of respectful behaviors begins at preschool age. On the other hand, at least it should.**

**Learning to appreciate other people's boundaries and differences rather than fear them.**

**One must show basic levels of empathy, honor, and values towards another person's belongings.**

## Eye affirm that all life is sacred

**Sacred: Spiritually connected to the Creator of All living things.**

**All created life is sacred. Human life especially has excellent value than all other life.**

**We must protect our fellow brothers and sister because that is of the utmost importance to our Creator.**

**All life should experience natural death.**

## Eye Give Offerings that are Genuine

**Offering: A thing offered as a gift or contribution but, not necessarily money. It can very well be giving of your time or level of ability free of charge.**

**Genuine: Sincere, honest, and truthful.**

**The offering should have the attributes of one's character.**

**It should be of quality rather than quantity. It is real and exact. Not fake or phony.**

**Never give under pretenses or with hidden motives.**

## Eye Live in Truth

**Truth: Facts or Reality. The real fact quality or state about something is the truth.**

**Live in your truth no matter what that truth may be.**

**Whatever that is, it is your happiness.**

**Perhaps, learn to live by moral principles rather than doctrines. Life is more meaningful when living what you value.**

**Living in your truth means not lying or hiding who you are.**

**However, you do not have to show your business unless you are entirely comfortable with the individual you wish to tell.**

**Some things are on a need-to-know basis.**

**Remember, not everyone deserves a front seat in your life.**

## Eye regard the altar within with respect

**Regard: Consider or think of in a specific kind of way. Concern or attention for something**

**Alters: supply a place of sanctuary. Some are considered sacred places where energy and spirit live.**

**Respect and love also reside there. It perhaps can be viewed as a metaphor for the beauty and harmony that dwell at the center of your very existence.**

**A later is a place where the enhancement of one's power and spirituality grows.**

**It positively changes your life.**

**Your Life should become a alter, a
light exuding peace and love to all.**

## Eye Speak Sincerity

**Sincerity: The quality of being free from pretense, or hypocrisy. Living a life of sincerity allows one to speak with conviction. Your delivery should be firm yet gentle.**

**Be natural, yet forceful; a combination of thought and strong feelings expressing your personality. Aim to master your subject of discussion. It will give you confidence as you speak. Understanding your topic of discussion will stimulate your audience's enthusiasm to listen to you.**

## Eye Consume Only My Fair Share

**Consume: To use or expend. To use up or spend what is necessary for you.**

**Live your life free from desiring favoritism or desired self-interest, bias, or deceptive desires.**

**Always conform to ethical established standards or rules that are put into place.**

**Never work from a sense of entitlement, always if you deserve more than others, special favors without having worked, or any form of reciprocity, just because.**

## Eye Offer Words of Good Intent

**Intent: Speaking honestly with keen attention. An abstract operation performed on purpose.**

**Speaking friendly and non-judgmental or condemning words, when talking about the actions or conduct of another.**

**Always have your heart in the right place. Mean well.**

**REMEMBER: He/She who tries to destroy others' ability to succeed must know that destruction awaits at the gate of his/her success.**

## Eye Relate in Peace

**Relate: Communicate, report, or tell.**

**How you relate to others is a direct reflection of how you feel inwardly.**

**If you live a life of chaos and confusion then, that is how your conversation will be, very chaotic.**

**Live life peacefully, always in a Conscious state of mind.**

**You have a responsibility to communicate peacefully with others.**

## Eye Honor Animals with Reverence

**Reverence: Deep respect or appreciation tinged with awe**

**Many animals are used for a food source and for that alone, one should house a deep appreciation.**

**Thus, before eaten, perhaps, a gesture of respect (as a bow) of prayer probably should be offered.**

## Eye Can Be Trusted

**Trust: Firm belief in the reliability, ability, or strength of someone or something.**

**Living the life of a trustworthy individual means that you are dependable.**

**You do what you say you are going to do if you cannot always offer a reason.**

**Remain honorable in every situation.**

## Eye Care for The Earth

**Careful, not to make this into some liberal political issue…**

**Simply put, caring for the Earth acknowledges your gratitude to the Supreme Power and Creator of all.**

**From the ocean creatures, trees and fields, the moon and the stars, all bring gratitude to the Creator.**

**Therefore, we should never carelessly destroy the earth.**

## Eye Keep My Council

**Council: A body of people elected to manage affairs a branch of government**

**Live your life responsibly and "manage" your affairs. Manage your own personal and financial matters. Court affairs may require legal representation.**

**Your life should never be burdensome to others.**

## Eye Speak Positively of Others

There is life or death in the powerful words that you speak.

You can either bless another or curse them with the same tongue.

Speaking negatively with regards to others can damage the perceptions of the individual. It is also a direct reflection of the kind of person you are.

So, be mindful of the words you speak concerning others, whether, you are a mother, sister, daughter, son, or leader, etc.

## Eye Remain in Balance with My Emotions

**Balance: Stability or steadiness. Correct proportions.**

**Keeping your thoughts and feelings combined equally while feeling good about what you are doing.**

**Emotional balance requires that one see their life, mind, and spirit equally by choosing wisely, what you eat and give your focus.**

**Maintain a positive outlook on life.**

## Eye Am Trustful in My Relationships

**Trustworthiness: Deserving of trust, confidence, dependability, and reliability.**

**Trust is something that you must build into all relationships. For people in relationships, technology supplies a perfect platform to engage in infidelity-like behaviors.**

**With online flirtation that supplies instant gratification, it is easy to make it feel like infidelity did not happen. Do not cheat with your mind, body, or emotions.**

**Trust must be maintained, by minimizing suspicions that stir jealousy and paranoia. Hold purity in high esteem. Discuss the criteria for infidelity.**

**All should have a clear definition of what commitment and infidelity mean.**

## Eye Spread Joy

**Joy: Feelings of great happiness pleasure and delight.**

**Living a life, that projects certain cheerfulness.**

**Radiates with good laughter and humor in hopes to uplift everyone you encounter.**

**Joy is being initiative-taking, always being conscious of your thoughts towards yourself and others. How you respond to your thoughts, will, and emotions towards yourself and others can have a significant impact on your Joy positively or negatively.**

## Eye Do the Best Eye Can

**Whatever you do, always do it with a Spirit of Excellence.**

**Doing the best that one can doesn't mean that you will never fail. It says that you have put forth an honest effort to achieve the desired goal.**

**Failing affords one to get back up and try it again.**

**One must appreciate their efforts made.**

**Never accept defeat.**

**Get back up and try it again.**

## Eye Communicates with Compassion

**Communicating with compassion is simple...**

**Pay attention to the words you use and the context or way in which you use them.**

**It strengthens and deepens your relationships.**

**The key is... to remember this principle when someone triggers your fewer good emotions.**

**Try extremely hard not to become negative.**

**Always respond in love.**

**Even when someone is hopelessly rude, do not get defensive.**

**It is, far easier said, than done. Nevertheless, keep working on how you communicate your response.**

**Try pausing before you respond when approaching another with compassion and understanding.**

## Eye Listen to Opposing Opinions

**Opposing: In conflict or contrary, resistance.**

**Listening to another's opinion is part of the communication process. Often, disagreements happen.**

**It is best to be objective rather than respond in hostility.**

**Becoming combative only further stresses the communication process.**

**Try not to become influenced by personal feelings or interpretations.**

**There is always more than one interpretation of a thing.**

**Opinions are best if based on facts, not assumptions.**

## Eye Create Harmony

**Like-mindedness, peacefulness, unity, understanding, and agreement are all elements of Harmony.**

**Harmony consists of living life in an orderly fashion without destroying one another.**

**If Fish and Livestock can manage to live in harmony, so can humans.**

## Eye Invoke Laughter

**Invoke: Help or inspire, aid, or support.**

**Being a happy person with a good sense of humor can invoke laughter in others.**

**Politeness and gentle interaction could perhaps appeal to an individual and invoke a smile.**

**Being supportive, encouraging, and inspirational are just a few ways to invoke laughter.**

**It is always rewarding to see another person smile from this inside out.**

Eye Am Open to Love in Various
Forms

- **Philia: Is the love between
  two friends.**
- **Eros: This is the sense of
  being in love.**
- **Storge: Is Affection, love of
  family.**
- **Agape: Is
  UNCONDITIONAL love.**

**There are diverse kinds of love,
according to the Greeks in
relationships with a wide range of
people, friends, family, spouses,
strangers.**

**Nevertheless, Agape love is the most
important of them all.**

However, unconditional love requires one to be non-judgmental or condemning.

One must learn to Love without conditions or limitations because everybody has flaws.

There should NEVER be any circumstances necessary not to Love someone completely.

We must love the alcoholics, drug addicts, the LGBT community, etc., without prejudices.

Again, MAÀT teaches us to MAINTAIN THE PURITY OF ONE's OWN HEART.

No one should ever need a reason to or not love another individual.

Directly. Period.

**The sooner we as people learn and understand this concept, the better our lives and community will be.**

**Eye Love you.**

# Eye Am Forgiving

**Forgiving: Stop feeling angry toward someone because of an offense, flaw, or mistake.**

**Letting go of anger, blame, and resentments in hopes of returning to friendly relations are what forgiving is all about.**

**Carrying around anger, blame, and resentments doesn't hurt the other person more than it hurts you.**

**Many times, one may feel vindicated... in the soul-sucking resentment being carried around day by day.**

**Nevertheless, eventually, it only affects YOU.**

Holding someone hostage emotionally by not forgiving him or she only prolongs the process of forgiveness.

Opt to feel compassion, rather than pain and rage.

Let go of that grievous wrong or offense that someone has done to you and start living your life today the MAÀT way.

# Eye Am Kind

**Kind: The character or nature of a person**

*"If you want others to be happy, practice compassion. If you want to be happy, practice compassion."*

*~ Dalai Lama*

**There are many ways to express Kindness throughout your day.**

**You can start by saying "Good morning," "Please," "Thank you," and "You're welcome."**

**You can end by saying, "Good night." Kindness... can be expressed randomly or on purpose.**

**One could complement another.**

You could express gratitude, for someone or something.

Volunteer your time and services.

Randomly buy flowers, gifts, or a card for someone or from someone.

Refuse to be judgmental towards another no matter your differences and express kindness.

The list goes on.

Here is to kindness and extraordinary life!

## Eye Act Respectfully of Others

**Acting respectfully towards others is how you show honor and worth.**

**Behaving politely and considering other people's feelings, asking before you use, or taking something that belongs to another is being respectful.**

**Differences should not matter.**

**Everyone deserves respect. Showing regard to something or someone means being respectful.**

(Example: A child being entirely quiet during class while the teacher is teaching is respectful.)

## Eye Am Accepting of Others

**Acceptance: The process of being viewed and or receive as being adequate or suitable in "society," a group, or a club.**

**Being accepting of others requires one to put aside any prejudices, judgments, or condemnations. No one needs the approval to live his or her life.**

**Therefore, accepting others and their differences should be automatic. People of all shapes, sizes, colors, and gender should feel safe in your presence and their surroundings.**

## Eye Follow My Inner-Voice & Inner-Guidance

**Inner voice: Perhaps is a Semi-constant internal speech or verbal streams of spiritual consciousness thinking in words**

**Inner guidance: Right actions. Most profound is knowledge of what or what not to do.**

**Following your inner voice and inner guidance requires active listening.**

**Do not let the noise of others around you drown out your inner voice. The choice to follow your inner voice is yours.**

**Inner guidance or intuitiveness is perhaps your first instinct to follow when you begin to feel lost or**

confused about various aspects of Life.

Learn to trust your intuition.

## Eye Converse with Awareness

**Awareness: A level of consciousness or the ability to perceive, to feel, or be conscious of thoughts, emotion, events, objects, being aware of something**

**Awareness and consciousness go hand in hand.**

**Both keep you safe.**

**When facing challenges that feel overwhelming that leaves one craving acceptance, understanding, and solutions one, awareness knows how to gather information necessary to ease that pain and frustration.**

**It will allow you the opportunity to make the necessary changes for the better of your life.**

**Discernment can help you overcome many obstacles and any threat as well. Learn to cultivate this gift. It will help you in Life.**

## Eye Do Well or Right

**Doing good makes, one feel right.**

**Doing good or well has such a broad term and has many meanings, such meanings as, doing desirable things, doing what's healthy and confident, etc.**

**Simply put, it is the idea that "doing well" for others is like food for the soul.**

**It is good for you.**

## Eye Give Blessings or Blissfulness to Others

**Blessings: Contributing to someone's happiness, well-being, and prosperity.**

**Giving blessings that contribute to others' happiness, welfare and success is the highest form of love and favor. Purposefully, steering away from the "approval" aspect of the word "blessing," limits the religious overtones of this word that indicate one needs the approval to be happy or prosperous. It is not the case in this set of principles that are not religious.**

# Eye Keep the Waters Pure

**Pure: Clean, clear, H2O is essential for most animal and plant life.**

**However, the higher meaning of water speaks of higher wisdom and a universal undertone of purity and fertility.**

**Water is the source of life.**

**Life appears from the water. Babies are in a fluid like water before birth.**

**Water is the circulation of life.**

**Water is on the earth and our bodies.**

**Water takes on the form of whatever is holding it and moves in the path of least resistance.**

There is much to learn from the water.

Perhaps, whatever state you find yourself in to be content and go with the flow?

Water sustains life and should be kept free of debris, toxins, lead, etc.

We are to preserve ALL Life.

## Eye Speaks with Good Intent

**Intent: Speaking honestly with keen attention. An abstract operation performed on purpose.**

**Speaking friendly and non-judgmental or condemning words, when talking about the actions or conduct of another.**

**Reframe from being hurtful, curt, or offensive while speaking to others.**

**Always have your heart in the right place.**

**Mean well.**

## Eye praise the Goddess & the God

**Goddess: An African female deity believed to be the source of Life.**

**God: Deity. The Creator of All Living Creatures**

**This book is not about Western Cultures that take us from pleasure to pain when dealing with circumstances out of our control. Maát laws and ideas give us principles to live by that will make our outcome more victorious. Maximizing pleasurable things and minimizing painful ones.**

## Eye Am Humble

**Being or showing humility, modesty, or low estimate of your importance, or humbleness does not mean neglecting your own needs to satisfy another.**

**It merely means to consider another person's feelings, such as a wife, mother, or child when making decisions.**

**Having high self-control is the key to being humble.**

**Displaying conceit or arrogance is not being humble.**

## Eye Achieves with Integrity

**Integrity: is having a Moral character.**

**Integrity is a quality of being honest and upright on the inside, living one's life by a set of ethical principles.**

**Integrity is an action word and requires one to do something.**

**One must govern self accordingly with a life of honesty rather than a life of deception.**

## Eye Advance through My Abilities

**Abilities: Having the skills or means to do something or One's Capabilities.**

**One must have self-confidence.**

**You must believe in your abilities to advance in this world. It doesn't matter how many "Nos'" you get, keep applying yourself until you get a "Yes."**

**Knowing your strengths and weaknesses will help you target areas in your life that need your attention.**

**Understanding the importance of self-reliance is the key.**

**Trusting that whatever happens in your life, good, bad, or indifferent**

you will be able to manage it
perhaps while practicing Maát.

## Eye Embrace the ALL

**Embracing ALL means to welcome with open arms the whole without limits or limitations of everything created, including, but not limited to people, places, and things without judgment or prejudices.**

**Accepting and supporting willingly, and enthusiastically.**

**Embrace without resistance.**

## Eye Hold Purity in High Esteem

**Purity: Freedom from immorality. Virtuous, cleanliness, freedom from contamination**

**Purity is a characteristic in the heart, mind-body, and soul.**

**Purity should manifest from the inside out as in moral conduct.**

**Meaning good morals and values should always be present and exercised. Holding someone or something, in high esteem or regard means that you respect him, or her worth or the value of a thing which could be a wife, girlfriend, mother, or child.**

# MAÀT 42 PLUS GOD

*Human beings who deviate from MAÀT will likely meet with frustration, anxiety, pain, and sorrow.*

## AUTHORS FINAL THOUGHT

**Now that you have read the basics, use this book as a catalyst to do your own research.**

**PLEASE, DON'T WORRY ABOUT GRAMMATICAL ERRORS. FOCUS ON RECEIVING THE MESSAGE.**

**MAÀT 42 PLUS GOD, written as a tool of enlightenment for those who are currently under the auspices of traditional religion, in hopes to expose the brainwashing that has occurred many generations ago that forced religion upon masses of people, by way of trauma, particularly of African Descent.**

**One will never understand the extent of the brainwashing until the topic of**

religious indoctrination is addressed in laymen's terms.

You cannot instruct a child about Calculus until you first teach them about addition.

Since I was raised a devout Christian, but no longer practice, I will address Christianity.

No, I Am Not an Atheist. Spirituality is my birthright and more of what I embrace, and not "Religion" that was forcefully taught to my great-great-grandmother, who trickled down throughout the generations to me.

My choice to denounce Christianity was to find a form of Spirituality less debilitating, and more liberating.

Once I began my studies in religion and philosophy, and at the same time collecting my research into what would later become this book about African Spirituality and Kemetic Spirituality, it was quite clear that I was on the righteous path seeking understanding.

Although it is essential to understand all religious teachings in the context of Human literature, Historical, Cultural, and Social Development to promote a greater overstanding for the advancement of humanity, deep down inside, I knew that IF the "God" was real, it was supposed to resemble me, one of African descent.

However, the one forced upon my Ancestors was European, with blue eyes and blonde hair. I did not have to be a historian to figure that one out.

So, I began my journey to find my true heritage, identity, and spirituality that complimented the essence of who I Am, inside and out.

During my quest for facts, I came to understand that Africans had a divine, and devoted spirituality, a philosophy that was the basis of Ancient Sages.

MAÀT is a cosmic force and a living social doctrine, which promotes social harmony to pave the way for Spiritual evolution today.

MAÀT is much like the Ten Commandments, which were stolen from these very same principles.

However, slaves were forced to engage in Christianity by the same people who beat raped, and tortured people of African descent. The oppressors raped and tortured people of African descent, Monday through Saturday, and on Sunday gave them Jesus.

The Savior of this religion is called, "Christianity."

How absurd is this?

Would someone who lynched, raped, tortured, and broke up African families, give you a Religion that is going to uplift, encourage, and empower you in any shape form, or fashion?

Let me help you with this answer. No!

A system was created to keep people of African Descent docile and in mental bondage for hundreds of years.

It was called Willie Lynch Syndrome, a letter that some would say is "Fake," but there is no way it could be because; it is still in full effect as I author this book.

Anyhow, Willie Lynch in the 1800s went from plantation to plantation, giving slave masters methods on how to keep slaves in check, and under complete and utter control, mentally, emotionally, and spiritually for many centuries to come.

Even to hate each other for two hundred plus years keeping them enslaved mentally.

Willie Lynch spoke very highly of King James, the man that inspired your Bible. Oh yes, it is true.

Do you think that they could conspire to keep you, the Christian, in bondage, and enslaved mentally?

It is very possible.

The Bible does CONDONE slavery, and it is time to tell your pastors to STOP cherry-picking scriptures to keep you a comfortable slave.

One cannot just read one scripture and ignore the rest of them. Stop making excuses for the buffoonery.

Read: Ephesians 6:5

Religion and the Scripture are debilitating to people of African descent in more ways than twenty.

It was designed to make you treat the Europeans like "Christ" because; subconsciously it associates the White man as "God" and Christ.

The Willie Lynch tactics are used to dummy down people of African descent to think that the White man is superior and the Black man inferior.

What a downer to know that your Bible condoned the elevating of one over the other.

Did it ever occur to you to ask "God," who's prayer would be answered first?

Since the slave and the slave master are praying to the same God… whose prayer would be answered.

Slaves wanted freedom, and the slave masters wanted obedient slaves.

For centuries, our ancestors were forced to pray to "God," as a being and not a Divine Vibratory Frequency.

They were removed from their land, culture, cuisine, families, and spirituality and given "Jesus," a blonde-haired, blue-eyed European who also resembled the slave master?

*"I am saying every single thing that touches your life, religiously, socially, and politically must be an instrument of your liberation or you must throw it in the trash can of history." - Dr. John Henrik Clarke*

It does not get any better than this.

In 1705, there was a law written in the Virginia Slave Code Act, which states, and I will paraphrase:

"Any person shipped over from a Christian country was to be a servant. This servant was to have decent food, clothing, and shelter and they were not to be whipped naked.

If they were to be whipped naked, the slave master had to compensate the slave.

The same law states:

"Any person shipped over from a non-Christian country, which would be people of African descent, you would convert into Christianity.

Mothers who would raise their children to be Christians posed a question; will you accept my child as being free, since I have grown them from an infant to be "Christian?"

Of course, the answer was, No.

So, they made another Law, in the Virginia Slave Code Act which stated:

"Christianity" will "Not" bring you freedom. Nor will you or your child be exempt from punishment.

(What a mind-blower!)

So basically, the fair exchange was a robbery.

Again, the question is still.

"Are you serving the "God" who you say you are serving within this Religion, given of white men?"

The sooner you Innerstand this, the more enlightened you will become.

There are many different Religions around the entire world.

Have you ever wondered why if there is only "One God," why so many different Religions?

It is the cause of so much division amongst people of African descent because; we are everywhere when it comes to Religion.

Other cultures practice their Religion. While people of African Descent, are confused because they did not come from "Religion," but from Spirituality.

If you believe that "Christianity" is the "Religion" of people of African Descent, then subconsciously you are grateful for Slavery and Racism.

If there were no slavery, people of African descent would not be "Christian."

Think about the Ancestors who were lynched who have transitioned to this place "Christianity" calls "Heaven" … and the Slavemaster who also transitioned. Do you honestly "think" that both are up in "Heaven?"

If so, how?

This Religious jargon does not add up.

You were beaten and taught never to question this belief because they knew this buffoonery did not add up.

You were taught to "Wait" for the reward that was supposed to be given to you when you reached this place called "Heaven," while white supremacists reap their reward right here on earth.

Why must you suffer, and they not have to suffer?

That is your logic with your Religion "Christianity."

This book was NOT written to offend OR convert anyone.

It was written to perhaps enlighten you and encourage you to THINK.

Not necessarily like the Author, but rather... just to THINK.

It was written with common sense, discernment, a little research, and a will to live a happier and enriched life full of prosperity and goodness, and a desire to share the knowledge with others. Ase`

When Truth is wrong, intellect is of no use. When Truth is correct, intellect is of no need. For the Numerology scholars, Maat resonates with the number 8, hence the fact, it's time for a new beginning of embracing righteous knowledge.

It's time out for being a toxic individual, creating chaos without a balance of order, pointing fingers, shifting blame, and avoiding taking responsibility.

Religion is like a hijacker of your divine DNA. It's time for self-healing.

## PRAYER TO THE GODDESS SEKHMET

I respectfully request your aid in helping me to become more assertive in my life, and to practice Self-healing, a Gift that I have instilled in me.

I ask that you provide me with guidance and support in learning how to develop qualities and apply principles in my life that it is beneficial and doesn't harm anyone.

En Sekhmet, het nebet no fret wabet

(To Sekhmet, all things are pure and beautiful)


Maat Ankhu Maat means:

"Maat is the Source of Life."

Maat Neb bu ten means:

"Maat is everywhere you are."

Cha hena Maat means:

"Rise in the morning with Maat."

**Ankh hena Maat means:**

**"Live with Maat."**

**Ha sema Maat means:**

**"Let every limb join with Maat and let her guide your actions.**

**Maat her ten means:**

**"Maat is who you are deep down inside."**

**Due Maat neb bu ten means"**
**"Adorations to Maat who is in everywhere you are."**

**Asé**

Author
LaTonya Page-Balkcom

# IF THIS BOOK RESONATED WITH YOUR "GOD" FREQUENCY...

# PLEASE, REVIEW THIS BOOK

# I LOVE YOU.

# MAÀT 42 PLUS GOD

**Truth, Justice, Order, Balance, Harmony, Reciprocity, and Love**

**PLEASE RETURN TO AMAZON**

**OR MY SECURE WEBSITE.**

**BOOK REVIEWS ARE WELCOMED**

**WWW.MAAT42PLUSGOD.COM**

**OR EMAIL YOUR REVIEW:**

**MAAT42PLUSGOD@YAHOO.COM**

FOR AFROTERIC APPAREL

HOODIES & T-SHIRTS

WWW.AFROTERICLOGODESIGNS.COM

I APPRECIATE YOUR SUPPORT.

## ABOUT THE AUTHOR

**L.P. Balkcom is a brilliant Afro-American self-published author based out of Illinois.**

**L.P. Balkcom is a loving mother of one child and grandmother of five loving children.**

**L.P. Balkcom officially started her writing career as a hobby in the late nineties with a focus on a Romance/Drama Novella.**

**Then later in Life, as she researched and studied alternatives to institutionalized Religion, she shifted and focused writings on Ancient Kemetic Spirituality.**

**Understanding the 42 Negative Confessions/Concepts or Principles of MAÀT, where she began her studies in the area of religion and**

philosophy, and at the same time collecting her research into what would later become this book, MAÀT 42 PLUS GOD, on the subject of African Spirituality and Kemetic Spirituality.

Although she believes it is essential to understand all religious teachings in the context of Human historical, cultural, and Social Development.

To promote a greater overstanding for the advancement of humanity, she gravitated towards the concept of MAÀT which existed 2000 years before the Ten Commandments, that Ancient African Ancestors practiced as a Spiritual People, in hopes to enlighten Melanated People and others.

**MAÀT is not a Religion, but merely a way of Life.**

**In May of 2015, she self-published her first adult book titled MAÀT 42 Plus God, and by "God" she means, the totality of Creation itself, followed by Colors of Consciousness and many more Books, which are all now available on her website: WWW.MAAT42PLUSGOD.COM, Amazon, Kindle, Create-space and Barnes & Noble, etc., as a Paperback book or e-book.**

**What inspired Latonya to write her "Best Seller" MAÀT 42 Plus GOD?**

**Growing up under the auspices of condemnation and judgments of Institutionalized Religion, which**

inhibited her from living a happy life, just being her unique and authentic Self. She began her search for Spirituality less debilitating and came across the teachings of MAÀT, Ancient Kemetic Concepts of Truth, Justice, Reciprocity, Balance, Order, and harmony. She began to practice & apply the 42 Principles of Ma'at, and her Spiritual life flourished in many positive ways.

It was her reintroduction to what blossomed from African Spirituality, rather than falsehoods that misrepresent true Spirituality.

L.P. Balkcom's book " MAÀT 42 Plus GOD," is NOT a Scholarly History Lesson, but rather to be perhaps considered a "Heart Lesson."

African spirituality did not condemn others but, instead, it stressed maintaining the purity of your own heart. Ase'

LaTonya, Writer/Author, has always felt that her determination as a writer would have a profound impact on the Publishing World and it has.

She offers Books for Adults and Children with topics that encourage self-awareness, self-expression, and self-determination by promoting Spirituality combined with self-empowerment that will perhaps guide others to Living a Balanced & Prosperous Life.

From Pain to Prestige, Author L.P. Balkcom is brilliant, smart, witty, self-taught, and well versed on many

**subjects, always collaborating with a Spirit of Excellence and Discernment; Latonya desires to become the next World-Renowned Author, for a new generation of readers.**

## CONTACT

**If you would like to offer a book deal
or invite:
Author Latonya Page-Balkcom
to your special event, please text:
971-378-4127
or email:
maat42plusgod@yahoo.com**

**PLEASE RETURN TO AMAZON** BOOK
**REVIEWS ARE WELCOMED**
www.amazon.com/-/e/B00ZPUYXF8

**OR VISIT MY SECURE WEBSITE TO
PURCHASE OR LEAVE A REVIEW:
WWW.MAAT42PLUSGOD.COM**

# DEDICATION

**Dedicated to my mom, Ernestine Jones-Page**

**Who deserved as much happiness as she could stand before she transitioned...?**

**April 18, 1991, R.I.P.**

**The blessings of the Lord, it maketh rich, and he addeth no sorrow with it ~ Proverbs 10:22 KJV**

**To My father**

**Herman Page Sr., for without you there would be no me**

**To my daughter Iiesha Ernestine Balkcom**

**For keeping me grounded**

**Also, to my grandchildren,**

**Mia Simone Smith, Martin (Marty) William Smith Jr., Ivy J. Latonia Trotman-Montoya, my namesake, Constance Joy Trotman, and Quentin Carter Trotman**

**You ALL are my inspiration**

**ALSO, BY WRITTEN BY**

**AUTHOR LATONYA PAGE-BALKCOM**


**AKASHA & YOU**

**REWIRE THE BLACK MIND TO PROSPER**

**RESIDUAL EFFECTS OF SLAVERY**

**BLACK NATIONHOOD**

**COLORS OF CONSCIOUSNESS**

**NO MORE HOOKUPS**

**WORDS OF A POETIC GODDESS**

**BLACK ENVY, BLACK JEALOUSY**


# FICTION/DRAMA/ROMANCE

**3 in One**

**THRESHOLD OF THE SOUL**

# 3 Book Series

## SPIRIT OF REJECTION Book 1

## SPIRIT OF LESBIANISM Book 2

## FROM PAIN TO PRESTIGE Book 3

# CHILDREN'S BOOK

## MIC-KEY, MS. PENELOPE & ME

## ANCIENT EGYPTIAN GODS, MYTHS & SYMBOLS

## SPIRIT-LED APPROACH TO PARENTING

# ♀ GRAND RISINGS ♀

## DON'T FORGET THE BOOK REVIEW

### WWW.MAAT42PLUSGOD.COM

## ... ON AMAZON TOO!

# STAY POSITIVE

Made in the USA
Middletown, DE
30 September 2023